RC Fashion

Casual dressing has never looked so good! These light and lacy designs were crocheted using Caron® Spa, a silky, multi-ply blend of bamboo and acrylic. The lustrous finish and superior drape of this exciting new yarn gives these four feminine fashions a dressy, go-everywhere flair. Crochet a cardigan, a pretty pullover, or a breezy tunic to refresh your warm-weather wardrobe.

Leisure Arts, Inc.
Little Rock, Arkansas

CandiDot Lace Shell

Shown on front cover.

■■■▢ **INTERMEDIATE**

Finished Size: Small{Medium-Large-Extra Large}
Finished Chest Measurement:
32{36-40-44}"/81{91.5-101.5-112} cm

Size Note: Instructions are written for size Small with sizes Medium, Large, and Extra Large in braces { }. Instructions will be easier to read if you circle all the numbers pertaining to your size. If only one number is given, it applies to all sizes.

MATERIALS

Caron® Spa
[3 ounces, 251 yards (85 grams, 230 meters) per skein]:
0008 Misty Taupe – 3{4-5-6} skeins
0002 Coral Lipstick (A) – 1 skein
0003 Soft Sunshine (B) – 1 skein
0004 Green Sheen (C) – 1 skein
0005 Ocean Spray (D) – 1 skein
Crochet hook, size G (4 mm) **or** size needed for gauge
Yarn needle

GAUGE: Rnds 1-5 of Motif = 4" (10 cm) square.
Each Motif = 4{4$\frac{1}{2}$-5-5$\frac{1}{2}$}"/ 10{11.5-12.75-14} cm

STITCH GUIDE

CLUSTER

YO, insert hook in st or sp indicated and pull up a loop, YO and draw through 2 loops on hook, ★ YO, insert hook in **same** st and pull up a loop, YO and draw through 2 loops on hook; repeat from ★ once **more**, YO and draw through all 4 loops on hook.

BEGINNING CLUSTER

Ch 3, ★ YO, insert hook in **same** st and pull up a loop, YO and draw through 2 loops on hook; repeat from ★ once **more**, YO and draw through all 3 loops on hook.

CORNER CLUSTER

★ YO, insert hook in **next** Cluster and pull up a loop, YO and draw through 2 loops on hook, YO, insert hook in **same** stitch and pull up a loop, YO and draw through 2 loops on hook; repeat from ★ once **more**, YO and draw through all 5 loops on hook.

Note: Garment is worked one Motif at a time, joining each Motif to the previous Motif(s) on the final round.

FIRST MOTIF

With Color A, ch 4; join with slip st to form a ring.

Rnd 1 (Right side)**:** Ch 3, [YO, insert hook in ring and pull up a loop, YO and draw through 2 loops on hook] twice, YO and draw through all 3 loops on hook, ch 2, ★ work Cluster in ring, ch 2; repeat from ★ 6 times **more**; join with slip st to top of first st, finish off: 8 sts and 8 ch-2 sps.

Note: Loop a short piece of yarn around any stitch to mark Rnd 1 as **right** side.

Rnd 2: With **right** side facing, join Misty Taupe with slip st in any st; ch 3, dc in same st, ch 4, sc in next ch-2 sp, ch 4, ★ work Corner Cluster, ch 4, sc in next ch-2 sp, ch 4; repeat from ★ 2 times **more**, YO, insert hook in next Cluster and pull up a loop, YO and draw through 2 loops on hook, YO, insert hook in **same** st and pull up a loop, YO and draw through 2 loops on hook, insert hook into top of first dc, YO and draw through st and all 3 loops on hook.

Rnd 3: Work Beginning Cluster, (ch 3, sc in next ch-4 sp) twice, ch 3, ★ work Cluster in next Corner Cluster, (ch 3, sc in next ch-4 sp) twice, ch 3; repeat from ★ around; join with slip st to Beginning Cluster.

Rnd 4: Work Beginning Cluster, (ch 4, sc in next ch-3 sp) 3 times, ch 4, ★ work Cluster in next Cluster, (ch 4, sc in next ch-3 sp) 3 times, ch 4; repeat from ★ around: join with slip st to Beginning Cluster.

Rnd 5: Work Beginning Cluster, (ch 5, sc in next ch-4 sp) 4 times, ch 5, ★ work Cluster in next Cluster, (ch 5, sc in next ch-4 sp) 4 times, ch 5; repeat from ★ around; join with slip st to Beginning Cluster.

Size Small Only: Finish off.

Rnd 6: Work Beginning Cluster, (ch 6, sc in next ch-5 sp) 5 times, ch 6, ★ work Cluster in next Cluster, (ch 6, sc in next ch-5 sp) 5 times, ch 6; repeat from ★ around; join with slip st to Beginning Cluster.

Size Medium Only: Finish off.

Rnd 7: Work Beginning Cluster, (ch 7, sc in next ch-6 sp) 6 times, ch 7, ★ work Cluster in next Cluster, (ch 7, sc in next ch-6 sp) 6 times, ch 7; repeat from ★ around; join with slip st to Beginning Cluster.

Size Large Only: Finish off.

Rnd 8: Work Beginning Cluster, (ch 8, sc in next ch-7 sp) 7 times, ch 8, ★ work Cluster in next Cluster, (ch 8, sc in next ch-7 sp) 7 times, ch 8; repeat from ★ around; join with slip st to Beginning Cluster, finish off.

ADDITIONAL MOTIFS

Following Placement Diagram, page 6, for color of Rnd 1, work same as First Motif through Rnd 4{5-6-7}; do **not** finish off.

Work One, Two or Three Side Joining.

ONE SIDE JOINING

Work Beginning Cluster, ★ [ch 5{6-7-8}, sc in next ch-sp] 4{5-6-7} times, ch 5{6-7-8}, work Cluster in next Cluster; repeat from ★ 2 times **more**, holding Motifs with **wrong** sides together, ch 2{3-3-4}, drop loop from hook, insert hook from **front** to **back** through corresponding ch-sp on **previous** Motif and pick up dropped loop, ch 3{3-4-4}, † sc in next ch-sp of **new** Motif, ch 2{3-3-4}, drop loop from hook, insert hook from **front** to **back** through corresponding ch-sp on **previous** Motif and pick up dropped loop, ch 3{3-4-4} †; repeat from † to † across; join with slip st to Beginning Cluster, finish off.

TWO SIDE JOINING

Work Beginning Cluster, ★ [ch 5{6-7-8}, sc in next ch-sp] 4{5-6-7} times, ch 5{6-7-8}, work Cluster in next Cluster; repeat from ★ once **more**, holding Motifs with **wrong** sides together, ch 2{3-3-4}, drop loop from hook, insert hook from **front** to **back** through corresponding ch-sp on **previous** Motif and pick up dropped loop, ch 3{3-4-4}, † sc in next ch-sp of **new** Motif, ch 2{3-3-4}, drop loop from hook, insert hook from **front** to **back** through corresponding ch-sp on **previous** Motif and pick up dropped loop, ch 3{3-4-4} †; repeat from † to † across to next Cluster on **new** Motif, work Cluster in next Cluster, ch 2{3-3-4}, drop loop from hook, insert hook from **front** to **back** through corresponding ch-sp on **previous** Motif and pick up dropped loop, ch 3{3-4-4}, repeat from † to † across; join with slip st to Beginning Cluster, finish off.

THREE SIDE JOINING

Work Beginning Cluster, [ch 5{6-7-8}, sc in next ch-sp] 4{5-6-7} times, ch 5{6-7-8}, work Cluster in next Cluster, holding Motifs with **wrong** sides together, ch 2{3-3-4}, drop loop from hook, insert hook from **front** to **back** through corresponding ch-sp on **previous** Motif and pick up dropped loop, ch 3{3-4-4}, † sc in next ch-sp of **new** Motif, ch 2{3-3-4}, drop loop from hook, insert hook from **front** to **back** through corresponding ch-sp on **previous** Motif and pick up dropped loop, ch 3{3-4-4} †; repeat from † to † across to next Cluster on **new** Motif, ★ work Cluster in next Cluster, ch 2{3-3-4}, drop loop from hook, insert hook from **front** to **back** through corresponding ch-sp on **previous** Motif and pick up dropped loop, ch 3{3-4-4}, repeat from † to † across to next Cluster on **new** Motif; repeat from ★ once **more**; join with slip st to Beginning Cluster, finish off.

FINISHING
NECK EDGING

Rnd 1: With **right** side facing join Misty Taupe with slip st in Cluster at point A; ch 3 **(counts as dc)**, dc in Cluster on next Motif, † ch 3{4-5-5}, [sc in next ch-sp, ch 3{4-5-5}] across to next Cluster, ★ sc in next Cluster, ch 3, [YO, insert hook in next Cluster on next Motif and pull up a loop, YO and draw through 2 loops on hook] twice, YO and draw through all 3 loops on hook, [ch 3{4-5-5}, sc in next ch-sp] across to next Cluster †, ch 3{4-5-5}; repeat from ★ once **more**, [YO, insert hook in next Cluster on next Motif and pull up a loop, YO and draw through 2 loops on hook] twice, YO and draw through all 3 loops on hook, repeat from † to † once, ch 0{1-1-2} **(see Zeros, page 30)**, dc in top of first dc to form last sp.

Rnd 2: Ch 1, sc in same sp, ★ ch 3{4-5-5}, sc in next ch-sp; repeat from ★ around, ch 0{1-1-2}, dc in first sc to form last sp.

Rnd 3: Repeat Rnd 2, decreasing chs at corners to keep piece lying flat; finish off.

Underarm Joining: With **right** side facing, join Misty Taupe with slip st in any Cluster at junction of Motifs at underarm; ch 1, sc in same Cluster, ch 3{4-5-5}, ★ sc in next Cluster, ch 3{4-5-5}; repeat from ★ 4 times **more**; join with slip st to first sc, finish off.

Repeat for second underarm.

Design by Edie Eckman.

PLACEMENT DIAGRAM

When joining motifs at sides with 3-side joining, match each Side Edge D to Edge C; when joining at underarm seams, match each Sleeve Edge A to Edge B.

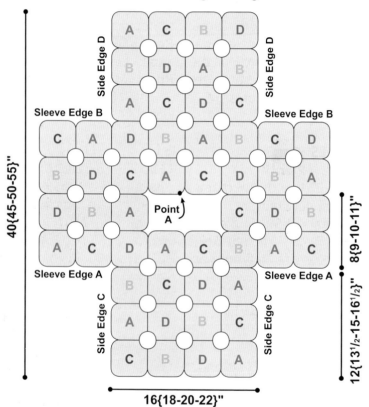

PLACEMENT DIAGRAM KEY:
A = CORAL LIPSTICK   C = GREEN SHEEN
B = SOFT SUNSHINE   D = OCEAN SPRAY

Casual Stripe Tunic

Shown on page 9.

■■■▢ **INTERMEDIATE**

Finished Size: Small{Medium-Large-Extra Large}
Finished Chest Measurement:
41{43³/₄-46¹/₂-51}"/104{111-118-129.5} cm

Size Note: Instructions are written for size Small with sizes Medium, Large, and Extra Large in braces { }. Instructions will be easier to read if you circle all the numbers pertaining to your size. If only one number is given, it applies to all sizes.

MATERIALS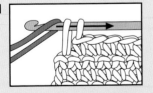

Caron® Spa
[3 ounces, 251 yards (85 grams, 230 meters) per skein]:
0007 Natural – 4{5-6-6} skeins
0008 Misty Taupe – 4{4-5-6} skeins
Crochet hook, size H (5 mm) **or** size needed for gauge
Yarn needle
Sewing needle and matching thread

GAUGE: In pattern, 15 sts and 17 rows = 4" (10 cm)

Gauge Swatch: 4" (10 cm) square
Ch 16.
Row 1: Sc in second ch from hook and each ch across: 15 sc.

Row 2: Ch 1, turn; sc in first sc, ★ ch 1, skip next sc, sc in next sc; repeat from ★ across.
Row 3: Ch 1, turn; sc in each sc and in each ch-1 sp across.
Rows 4-17: Repeat Rows 2 and 3, 7 times.
Finish off.

STITCH GUIDE
CHANGING COLORS
Work the last stitch to within one step of completion, hook new yarn *(Fig. 1)* and draw through all loops on hook. Do **not** cut old yarn unless instructed.

Fig. 1

SINGLE CROCHET DECREASE
(abbreviated sc dec)
Pull up a loop in each of next 2 stitches or spaces, YO and draw through all 3 loops on hook **(counts as one sc)**.

ADDING ON SINGLE CROCHETS

When instructed to add on sc at the end of a row, insert hook into base of last sc *(Fig. 2)*, YO and pull up a loop, YO and draw through one loop on hook, YO and draw through both loops on hook. Repeat as many times as instructed.

Fig. 2

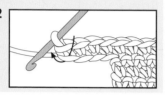

Note: Tunic is worked from side to side beginning with bottom edge of left sleeve. Front of tunic has more ease (extra rows) than the back.

LEFT SLEEVE

With Natural, ch 82.

Row 1 (Right side)**:** Sc in second ch from hook and each ch across: 81 sc.

Note: Loop a short piece of yarn around any stitch to mark Row 1 as **right** side.

Row 2: Ch 1, turn; sc in first sc, ★ ch 1, skip next sc, sc in next sc; repeat from ★ across, changing to Misty Taupe in last sc: 41 sc and 40 ch-1 sps.

Row 3 (Increase row)**:** Ch 1, turn; 2 sc in first sc, sc in each sc and in each ch-1 sp across to last sc, 2 sc in last sc: 83 sc.

Row 4: Ch 1, turn; sc in first sc, ★ ch 1, skip next sc, sc in next sc; repeat from ★ across, changing to Natural in last sc: 42 sc and 41 ch-1 sps.

Row 5: Ch 1, turn; sc in each sc and in each ch-1 sp across: 83 sc.

Rows 6-33: Repeat Rows 2-5, 7 times: 97 sc.

Row 34: Ch 1, turn; slip st in first 10 sc, sc in next sc, ★ ch 1, skip next sc, sc in next sc; repeat from ★ across to last 10 sc, slip st in last 10 sc, changing to Misty Taupe in last st: 20 slip sts, 39 sc, and 38 ch-1 sps.

Row 35 (Increase row)**:** Ch 1, turn; working first and last 10 sts in row **below** (same sts as slip sts), 2 sc in first st, sc in each st and in each ch-1 sp across to last st, 2 sc in last st: 99 sc.

Row 36: Ch 1, turn; sc in first sc, ★ ch 1, skip next sc, sc in next sc; repeat from ★ across, changing to Natural in last sc.

Row 37: Ch 1, turn; working in sc and in ch-1 sps, sc in first 38 sts, hdc in next 23 sts, sc in each st across: 76 sc and 23 hdc.

Row 38: Ch 1, turn; slip st in first 10 sc, sc in next sc, ★ ch 1, skip next st, sc in next st; repeat from ★ across to last 10 sc, slip st in last 10 sc, changing to Misty Taupe in last sc: 20 slip sts, 40 sc, and 39 ch-1 sps.

Row 39 (Increase row)**:** Ch 1, turn; working first and last 10 sc in row **below** and in sc and ch-1 sps, 2 sc in first st, sc in next 37 sts, hdc in next 23 sts, sc in each st across to last st, 2 sc in last st: 78 sc and 23 hdc.

Rows 40-69: Repeat Rows 36-39, 7 times; then repeat Rows 36 and 37 once **more**, working one more sc before and after center 23 hdc after each increase row: 115 sts.

LEFT SHOULDER AND BODY

Row 1 (Wrong side)**:** Ch 52, turn; sc in second ch from hook and in each ch across to Sleeve, sc in next st, ★ ch 1, skip next st, sc in next st; repeat from ★ across, add on 51 sc, changing to Misty Taupe in last sc: 217 sc.

Row 2: Ch 1, turn; sc in each sc and in each ch-1 sp across.

Row 3: Ch 1, turn; sc in first sc, ★ ch 1, skip next sc, sc in next sc; repeat from ★ across, changing to Natural in last sc.

Row 4: Ch 1, turn; sc in each sc and in each ch-1 sp across.

Row 5: Ch 1, turn; sc in first sc, ★ ch 1, skip next sc, sc in next sc; repeat from ★ across, changing to Misty Taupe in last sc.

Rows 6-17: Repeat Rows 2-5, 3 times.

BACK

Row 1 (Right side)**:** Ch 1, turn; 2 sc in first sc, working in sc and ch-1 sps, sc in next 107 sts, leave remaining sts unworked: 109 sc.

Row 2: Ch 1, turn; sc in first sc, ★ ch 1, skip next sc, sc in next sc; repeat from ★ across, changing to Natural in last sc: 55 sc and 54 ch-1 sps.

Row 3: Ch 1, turn; sc in each sc and in each ch-1 sp across.

Row 4: Ch 1, turn; sc in first sc, ★ ch 1, skip next sc, sc in next sc; repeat from ★ across, changing to Misty Taupe in last sc.

Row 5: Ch 1, turn; sc in each sc and in each ch-1 sp across.

Rows 6 thru 48{52-56-60}:
Repeat Rows 2-5, 10{11-12-13}
times, then repeat Rows 2-4
once **more**, do **not** change to
Natural at end of last row.

Finish off.

FRONT

Row 1: With **right** side facing,
skip next sc on last row of Left
Shoulder, join Misty Taupe with
sc in next sc **(see Joining with
Sc, page 31)**; working in sc and
ch-1 sps, sc in each st across to
last sc, 2 sc in last sc: 109 sc.

Row 2: Ch 1, turn; sc in first
sc, ★ ch 1, skip next sc, sc in
next sc; repeat from ★ across,
changing to Natural in last sc:
55 sc and 54 ch-1 sps.

Row 3: Ch 1, turn; sc in each sc
and in each ch-1 sp across.

Row 4: Ch 1, turn; sc in first
sc, ★ ch 1, skip next sc, sc in
next sc; repeat from ★ across,
changing to Misty Taupe in
last sc.

Row 5: Ch 1, turn; sc in each sc
and in each ch-1 sp across.

Rows 6 thru 27{31-35-39}:
Repeat Rows 2-5, 5{6-7-8}
times; then repeat Rows 2 and
3 once **more**.

Cut Misty Taupe.

Row 28{32-36-40} (Center
split)**:** Ch 1, turn; sc in first sc,
★ ch 1, skip next sc, sc in next
sc; repeat from ★ 39 times
more; leave remaining sts
unworked: 41 sc and
40 ch-1 sps.

Row 29{33-37-41}: With **right**
side facing, join Misty Taupe
with sc in first sc; sc in each
ch-1 sp and in each sc across:
109 sc.

Row 30{34-38-42}: Ch 1, turn;
sc in first sc, ★ ch 1, skip next
sc, sc in next sc; repeat from ★
across, add on 28 sc, changing
to Natural in last sc: 55 sc and
54 ch-1 sps.

Row 31{35-39-43}: Ch 1, turn;
sc in each sc and in each ch-1
sp across.

Row 32{36-40-44}: Ch 1, turn;
sc in first sc, ★ ch 1, skip next
sc, sc in next sc; repeat from ★
across, changing to Misty Taupe
in last sc.

Row 33{37-41-45}: Ch 1, turn,
sc in each sc and in each ch-1
sp across.

Rows 34{38-42-46}: Ch 1, turn,
sc in first sc, ★ ch 1, skip next
sc, sc in next sc; repeat from ★
across, changing to Natural in
last sc.

Rows 35{39-43-47} thru 56{64-72-80}: Repeat Rows 31{35-39-43} thru 34{38-42-46} 5{6-7-8} times; then repeat Rows 31{35-39-43} and 32{36-40-44} once **more**; do **not** change to Natural at end of last row.

Finish off.

RIGHT SHOULDER AND BODY

Row 1 With **right** side facing, join Misty Taupe with sc in first sc on Back; sc in each sc and in each ch-1 sp across Back, sc in each sc and in each ch-1 sp across right Front: 218 sc.

Row 2: Ch 1, turn; sc dec, ★ ch 1, skip next st, sc in next sc; repeat from ★ across, changing to Natural in last sc: 109 sc and 108 ch-1 sps.

Row 3: Ch 1, turn; sc in each sc and in each ch-1 sp across:217 sc.

Row 4: Ch 1, turn; sc in first sc, ★ ch 1, skip next sc, sc in next sc; repeat from ★ across, changing to Misty Taupe in last sc.

Row 5: Ch 1, turn; sc in each sc and in each ch-1 sp across.

Row 6: Ch 1, turn; sc in first sc, ★ ch 1, skip next sc, sc in next sc; repeat from ★ across, changing to Natural in last sc.

Rows 7-17: Repeat Rows 3-6 twice, then repeat Rows 3-5 once **more**.

Finish off.

RIGHT SLEEVE

Row 1: With **wrong** side facing, skip first 51 sc and join Misty Taupe with sc in next sc; ★ ch 1, skip next sc, sc in next sc; repeat from ★ 56 times **more**, leaving remaining sts unworked and changing to Natural in last sc: 58 sc and 57 ch-1 sps.

Row 2 (Decrease row): Ch 1, turn; working in sc and in ch-1 sps, sc dec, sc in next 44 sts, hdc in next 23 sts, sc in each st across to last 2 sts, sc dec: 90 sc and 23 hdc.

Row 3: Ch 1, turn; slip st in first 10 sc, sc in next sc, ★ ch 1, skip next st, sc in next st; repeat from ★ across to last 10 sc, slip st in last 10 sc, changing to Misty Taupe in last st: 20 slip sts, 47 sc, and 46 ch-1 sps.

Row 4: Ch 1, turn; working first and last 10 sts in row **below** and in sc and in ch-1 sps, sc in first 45 sts, hdc in next 23 sts, sc in each st across.

Row 5: Ch 1, turn; sc in first sc, ★ ch 1, skip next st, sc in next st; repeat from ★ across, changing to Natural in last sc.

Rows 6-37: Repeat Rows 2-5, 8 times, working one less sc before and after center 23 hdc after each decrease row: 97 sts.

Row 38 (Decrease row)**:** Ch 1, turn; sc dec, sc in each sc and in each ch-1 sp across to last 2 sts, sc dec: 95 sc.

Row 39: Ch 1, turn; sc in first sc, ★ ch 1, skip next sc, sc in next sc; repeat from ★ across, changing to Misty Taupe in last sc.

Row 40: Ch 1, turn; sc in each sc and in each ch-1 sp across.

Row 41: Ch 1, turn; sc in first sc, ★ ch 1, skip next sc, sc in next sc; repeat from ★ across, changing to Natural in last sc.

Rows 42-69: Repeat Rows 38-41, 7 times; do **not** change to Natural on last row: 81 sts.

Finish off.

FINISHING
SLEEVE SIDE EDGING
First Side: With **right** side facing, join Natural with sc in end of first row of Sleeve; sc in each row across, skipping rows ending with slip sts; finish off.

Second Side: With **right** side facing, join Natural with sc in end of last row of Sleeve; sc in each row across, skipping rows ending with slip sts.
Finish off.

Working through both loops of Sleeve Side Edging, whipstitch Sleeve seam *(Fig. 6b, page 31)*.

Repeat for second Sleeve.

Whipstitch side seams.

NECK EDGE
Row 1: With **right** side facing, join Natural with sc in Right Front at top of center split, sc evenly across to Back, sc dec evenly spaced across to Left Front, sc evenly across to top of center split.

Row 2: Ch 1, turn; slip st in each st across.

Finish off.

BOTTOM BAND

Rnd 1: Working in end of rows around bottom, join Natural with sc in either seam; sc in each row and seam around; join with slip st to first sc: 178{190-202-214} sc.

Rnd 2: Ch 1, ★ sc dec, ch 1, skip next st, [sc in next sc, ch 1, skip next sc] 43{45-47-49} times; repeat from ★ once **more**; join with slip st to first sc: 88{92-96-100} sts and 88{92-96-100} ch-1 sps.

Rnd 3: Ch 1, ★ sc dec, sc in next sc and in next ch-1 sp; repeat from ★ around; join with slip st to first sc: 132{138-144-150} sc.

Rnd 4: Ch 1, ★ sc in next sc, ch 1, skip next sc; repeat from ★ around, join with slip st to first sc.

Rnd 5: Ch 1, sc in each sc and in each ch-1 sp around; join with slip st to first sc.

Rnds 6-13: Repeat Rnds 4 and 5, 4 times.

Finish off.

Design by Tammy Hildebrand.

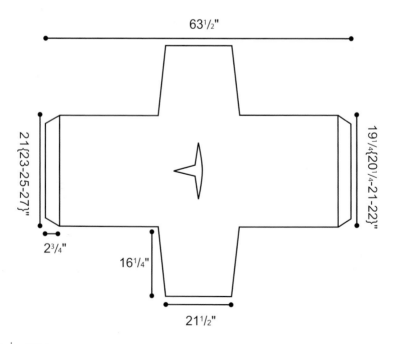

63¹/₂"

21{23-25-27}"

19¹/₄{20¹/₄-21-22}"

2³/₄"

16¹/₄"

21¹/₂"

Spider Web Lace Cardigan

Shown on page 17.

■■■◻ INTERMEDIATE

Finished Size: Small{Medium-Large/Extra Large-2X/3X}
Finished Chest Measurement:
36{45-54-63}"/91.5{114.5-137-160} cm

Size Note: Instructions are written for size Small with sizes Medium, Large/Extra Large, and 2X/3X in braces { }. Instructions will be easier to read if you circle all the numbers pertaining to your size. If only one number is given, it applies to all sizes.

MATERIALS

Caron® Spa
[3 ounces, 251 yards (85 grams, 230 meters) per skein]:
0004 Green Sheen – 4{5-6-6} skeins
Crochet hooks, sizes G (4 mm) **and** H (5 mm) **or** sizes needed for gauge
Stitch markers
Yarn needle

GAUGE: With smaller size hook, 2 pattern repeats = 4¹⁄₂" (11.5 cm) square

Gauge Swatch: 4¹⁄₂" x 5" (11.5 cm x 12.5 cm)
Ch 30.
Rows 1-14: Work same as Back.
Finish off.

STITCH GUIDE

DOUBLE CROCHET DECREASE (abbreviated dc dec)
★ YO, insert hook in **next** st, YO and pull up a loop, YO and draw through 2 loops on hook; repeat from ★ once **more**, YO and draw through all 3 loops on hook.

Notes: Cardigan is worked from bottom of back up to the shoulders. The piece then splits at neck and the fronts are worked separately. The sleeves are worked from side edges.

BACK
With smaller size hook, ch 114{142-170-198}.

Row 1 (Right side)**:** Sc in second ch from hook, ★ ch 4, skip next 3 chs, dc in next ch, (ch 1, skip next 2 chs, dc in next ch) twice, ch 4, skip next 3 chs, sc in next ch; repeat from ★ across.

Note: Loop a short piece of yarn around any stitch to mark Row 1 as **right** side.

Row 2: Ch 5 **(counts as first dc plus ch 2, now and throughout)**, turn; (dc, ch 2, dc) in next dc, dc in next dc, (dc, ch 2, dc) in next dc, ch 2, dc in next sc, ★ ch 2, (dc, ch 2, dc) in next dc, dc in next dc, (dc, ch 2, dc) in next dc, ch 2, dc in next sc; repeat from ★ across.

Row 3: Ch 5, turn; hdc in next dc, ch 2, sc in next dc, slip st in next dc, sc in next dc, ch 2, hdc in next dc, ch 2, dc in next dc, ★ ch 2, hdc in next dc, ch 2, sc in next dc, slip st in next dc, sc in next dc, ch 2, hdc in next dc, ch 2, dc in next dc; repeat from ★ across.

Row 4: Ch 5, turn; hdc in next hdc, ch 2, sc in next sc, ch 1, skip next slip st, sc in next sc, ch 2, hdc in next hdc, ch 2, dc in next dc, ★ ch 2, hdc in next hdc, ch 2, sc in next sc, ch 1, skip next slip st, sc in next sc, ch 2, hdc in next hdc, ch 2, dc in next dc; repeat from ★ across.

Row 5: Ch 7 **(counts as first dc plus ch 4)**, turn; dc dec, ch 1, dc in next ch-1 sp, ch 1, dc dec, ch 4, dc in next dc, ★ ch 4, dc dec, ch 1, dc in next ch-1 sp, ch 1, dc dec, ch 4, dc in next dc; repeat from ★ across.

Row 6: Ch 1, turn; sc in first dc, ★ ch 3, dc in next st, (ch 2, dc in next st) twice, ch 3, sc in dc; repeat from ★ across.

Row 7: Ch 1, turn; sc in first sc, ★ ch 4, dc in next dc, (ch 1, dc in next dc) twice, ch 4, sc in next sc; repeat from ★ across.

Repeat Rows 2-7, 4{5-5-6} times; then repeat Rows 2-6 once **more**. Place marker at each end of last row for Sleeve placement.

Next Row: Repeat Row 7.

Repeat Rows 2-7, 4{4-5-5} times **more**. Do **not** finish off.

RIGHT FRONT
Row 1: Ch 5, turn; (dc, ch 2, dc) in next dc, dc in next dc, (dc, ch 2, dc) in next dc, ch 2, dc in next sc, ★ ch 2, (dc, ch 2, dc) in next dc, dc in next dc, (dc, ch 2, dc) in next dc, ch 2, dc in next sc; repeat from ★ 1{2-3-4} times **more**, leave remaining sts unworked.

Rows 2-6: Repeat Rows 3-7 of Back.

Repeat Rows 2-7 of Back, 2{2-3-3} times; then repeat Rows 2-6 once **more**.

Place a marker at each end of last row to mark Sleeve placement.

Next Row: Repeat Row 7 of Back.

Repeat Rows 2-7 of Back, 6{7-7-8} times, then repeat Row 2 once **more**.

Finish off.

LEFT FRONT

With **wrong** side facing, skip next 8 ch-sps on last row of Back and join with slip st in next sc; ch 5, (dc, ch 2, dc) in next dc, dc in next dc, (dc, ch 2, dc) in next dc, ch 2, dc in next sc, ★ ch 2, (dc, ch 2, dc) in next dc, dc in next dc, (dc, ch 2, dc) in next dc, ch 2, dc in next sc; repeat from ★ across.

Complete same as Right Front, beginning with Row 2.

SLEEVES

Row 1: With **right** side facing and working in end of rows, join yarn with slip st at first marker; ch 1, sc in same st, ★ ch 4, skip next row, dc in next row, (ch 1, dc in next row) twice, ch 4, skip next row, sc in next row; repeat from ★ across to next marker.

Repeat Rows 2-7 of Back 2{2-2-3} times.

Finish off.

Repeat for second Sleeve.

FINISHING

Sew side and underarm seams.

RIGHT FRONT EDGING

Row 1: With **right** side facing and smaller size hook, join yarn with slip st in bottom corner; ch 4, (dc, ch 1) evenly spaced across to last 2 rows, dc dec.

Row 2: Ch 3, turn; dc in next dc, (ch 1, dc in next dc) across; finish off.

LEFT FRONT EDGING

With **wrong** side facing, join yarn with slip st in bottom corner; work same as Right Front Edging, do **not** finish off.

BODY EDGING

Rnd 1: Ch 4, (dc, ch 1) evenly around, working (dc, ch 1) twice in each corner; join with slip st to third ch of beginning ch-4.

Rnd 2: With larger size hook, ch 1; working from **left** to **right**, work reverse sc *(Figs. 4a-d, page 31)* in each ch-1 sp around; join with slip st to first st, finish off.

SLEEVE EDGING

Rnd 1: With **wrong** side facing and smaller size hook, join yarn with slip st at underarm seam; ch 4, (dc, ch 1) evenly around Sleeve edge; join with a slip st to third ch of beginning ch-4.

Rnd 2: Repeat Rnd 2 of Body Edging.

Repeat for second Sleeve.

Design by Karen Drouin.

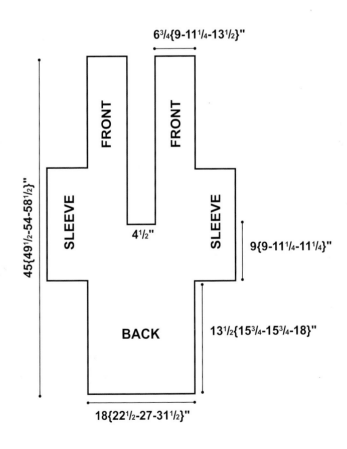

$6^3/_4${9-11$^1/_4$-13$^1/_2$}"

FRONT

FRONT

SLEEVE

SLEEVE

45{49$^1/_2$-54-58$^1/_2$}"

4$^1/_2$"

9{9-11$^1/_4$-11$^1/_4$}"

BACK

13$^1/_2${15$^3/_4$-15$^3/_4$-18}"

18{22$^1/_2$-27-31$^1/_2$}"

Breezy Lace Jacket

Shown on back cover.

◼◼◼◻ **INTERMEDIATE**

Finished Size: {Small-Medium-Large}{Extra Large-2X-3X}
Finished Chest Measurement:
{36-40-44}{48-52-56}"/{91.5-101.5-112}{122-132-142} cm

Size Note: Instructions are written for sizes Small, Medium, and Large in the first set of braces { } and sizes Extra Large, 2X, and 3X in the second set of braces. Instructions will be easier to read if you circle all the numbers pertaining to your size. If only one number is given, it applies to all sizes.

MATERIALS

LIGHT 3

Caron® Spa
[3 ounces, 251 yards (85 grams, 230 meters) per skein]:
0005 Ocean Spray – {6-7-8} {9-10-11} skeins
Crochet hook, size G (4 mm) **or** size needed for gauge
$^{11}/_{16}$" (18 mm) shank buttons - 3
Yarn needle
Sewing needle and matching thread.

GAUGE

Each Motif = 5$^{1}/_{2}$" (14 cm) square

STITCH GUIDE

CLUSTER

YO, insert hook in next st and pull up a loop, YO and draw through 2 loops on hook, YO, insert hook in **same** st and pull up a loop, YO and draw through 2 loops on hook, YO and draw through all 3 loops on hook.

MOTIF PANEL

Make {5-5-5}{7-7-7} panels of 3 Motifs each and 2 panels of 6 Motifs each.

FIRST MOTIF

Ch 5; join with slip st to form a ring.

Rnd 1 (Right side): Ch 1, 16 sc in ring; join with slip st to first sc: 16 sc.

Note: Loop a short piece of yarn around any stitch to mark Rnd 1 as **right** side.

Rnd 2: [Ch 3, dc in same st **(counts as first Cluster)**], ch 3, slip st in next sc, ch 3, ★ work Cluster in next sc, ch 3, slip st in next sc, ch 3; repeat from ★ around; join with slip st to first dc: 8 Clusters and 8 slip sts.

Rnd 3: Ch 1, sc in same st, ch 5, ★ sc in next Cluster, ch 5; repeat from ★ around; join with slip st to first sc: 8 sc and 8 ch-5 sps.

Rnd 4: Ch 1, sc in same st, ch 3, sc in next ch-5 sp, ch 3, ★ sc in next sc, ch 3, sc in next ch-5 sp, ch 3; repeat from ★ around; join with slip st to first sc: 16 sc and 16 ch-3 sps.

Rnd 5: Slip st in next ch-3 sp, ch 1, sc in same sp, ch 5, sc in next ch-3 sp, ch 3, ★ sc in next ch-3 sp, ch 5, sc in next ch-3 sp, ch 3; repeat from ★ around; join with slip st to first sc, finish off: 16 sc, 8 ch-3 sps, and 8 ch-5 sps.

ADDITIONAL MOTIFS
Work same as First Motif through Rnd 4.

Rnd 5: Slip st in next ch-3 sp, ch 1, sc in same sp, ★ ch 5, sc in next ch-3 sp, ch 3, sc in next ch-3 sp; repeat from ★ 5 times **more**, † ch 2, drop loop from hook, insert hook from **front** to **back** through corresponding ch-5 sp on **previous** Motif and pick up dropped loop †, (ch 3, sc in next ch-3 sp) twice, repeat from † to † once, ch 3, sc in next ch-3 sp, ch 3; join with slip st to first sc, finish off.

MOTIF PANEL BORDER
Rnd 1: With **right** side facing, join yarn with sc in center ch-3 sp at one end of Motif Panel **(see Joining With Sc, page 31)**; ch 5, (sc in next ch-sp, ch 5) 5 times, dc in next ch-3 sp, (tr, ch 3, tr) in Motif joining, dc in next ch-3 sp, † ch 5, (sc in next ch-sp, ch 5) 3 times, dc in next ch-3 sp, (tr, ch 3, tr) in Motif joining, dc in next ch-3 sp †; repeat from † to † across to last Motif, ch 5, (sc in next ch-sp, ch 5) 11 times, dc in next ch-3 sp, (tr, ch 3, tr) in Motif joining, dc in next ch-3 sp, repeat from † to † across to last Motif on second side of Motif Panel, ch 5, (sc in next ch-sp, ch 5) 5 times; join with slip st to first sc.

Rnd 2: Slip st in next 3 chs, ch 1, sc in same sp, ch 1, sc in next ch-5 sp, ch 1, † (3 dc, ch 3, 3 dc) in next ch-5 sp, ch 1, (3 dc in next ch-5 sp, ch 1) 3 times, (tr, ch 1, tr) in next ch-3 sp, ch 1, [(3 dc in next ch-5 sp, ch 1) 4 times, (tr, ch 1, tr) in next ch-3 sp, ch 1] across to last Motif, (3 dc in next ch-5 sp, ch 1) 3 times, (3 dc, ch 3, 3 dc) in next ch-5 sp †, (ch 1, sc in next ch-5 sp) 4 times, ch 1; repeat from † to † once, (ch 1, sc in next ch-5 sp) twice, ch 1; join with slip st to first sc.

Rnd 3: Ch 3 **(counts as first dc, now and throughout)**, ★ dc in each st and in each ch across to center ch of next corner ch-3, (dc, ch 1, dc) in center ch of corner; repeat from ★ 3 times **more**, dc in each st and in each ch across; join with slip st to top of beginning ch-3.

Rnd 4: Working in both loops of each dc and ch around, insert hook in next st from **front** to **back**, then insert hook in **next** st from **back** to **front** *(Fig. 3)*, YO and draw through loop on hook, ★ insert hook from **front** to **back** in **same** st, then insert hook from **back** to **front** in **next** st, YO and draw through loop on hook; repeat from ★ around; join with slip st to first st, finish off.

Note: Loop a short piece of yarn through one end of each Long Panel to mark bottom edge and Back. Mark one end of each Short Panel in same manner.

SIDE PANEL (Make 2)
Sizes Extra Large, 2X, and 3X Only
Work First Motif; do **not** finish off.

SIDE PANEL BORDER
Rnd 1: Slip st in next 3 chs, ch 1, sc in same sp, ch 5, (sc in next ch-sp, ch 5) around; join with slip st to first sc: 16 sc and 16 ch-5 sps.

Rnd 2: Slip st in next 3 chs, ch 1, sc in same sp, (ch 1, sc in next ch-5 sp) 3 times, place marker in last sc made to mark bottom edge, † ch 1, (3 dc, ch 3, 3 dc) in next ch-5 sp, ch 1, (3 dc in next ch-5 sp, ch 1) twice, (3 dc, ch 3, 3 dc) in next ch-5 sp †, (ch 1, sc in next ch-5 sp) 4 times, repeat from † to † once, ch 1; join with slip st to first sc: 36 dc and 8 sc.

Fig. 3

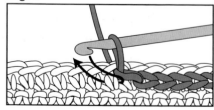

Rnds 3 and 4: Repeat Rnds 3 and 4 of Motif Panel Border.

PANEL EDGING

Row 1: With **right** side facing, working in back loops *(Fig. 5, page 31)* of Rnd 3 of Border, join yarn with sc in bottom right corner ch; sc in each st across to next corner ch, sc in corner ch: 21 sc.

Sizes Small, Medium, Large, and 2X Only
Finish off.

Sizes Extra Large and 3X Only
Row 2: Ch 1, turn; sc in both loops of each sc across; finish off.

All Sizes
Repeat on opposite edge.

BODY ASSEMBLY

Holding Panels with **wrong** sides together and matching bottom edges, and working through inside loops of each piece, whipstitch long edge of one marked Short Panel to Long Panel *(Fig. 6a, page 31)*.

Whipstitch second side of Short Panel to second Long Panel *(see Assembly Diagrams, this page and page 25)*.

LONG PANEL SIDE EDGING

With **right** side facing, working in back loops of Rnd 3 of Border, join yarn with sc in bottom right corner ch; sc in each st across to next corner ch, sc in corner ch; finish off: 121 sc.

SMALL, MEDIUM AND LARGE BODY ASSEMBLY

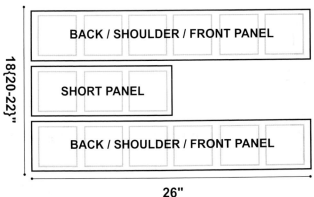

Sizes Extra Large, 2X, and 3X Only

Holding Panels with **wrong** sides together and working through inside loops of both pieces, whipstitch one Side Panel to outside bottom edge of each Long Panel.

Fold Long Panels in half and whipstitch opposite side of each Side Panel to opposite end of corresponding Long Panel in same manner, leaving center 79 sts open for sleeve.

Sizes Small, Medium, and Large Only

Fold Long Panel in half with **wrong** sides together. Working in inside loops, whipstitch first 30 sts together, leaving 61 sts open for sleeve. Repeat for second side.

PANEL FRONT AND NECK EDGING

Row 1: With **right** side facing, working in back loops only on Border Rnd 3, join yarn with sc in lower right corner ch on right front; sc in each st across to shoulder, skip ch-1 on Long Panel at shoulder, sc in each st across top of Short Panel, skip ch-1 on Long Panel, sc in each st across left front to corner, sc in left corner ch: 141 sc.

Sizes Medium, Large, 2X, and 3X Only

Row 2: Ch 3, turn; dc in both loops of each sc across: 141 dc.

Row 3: Ch 1, turn; working in back loops only, sc in each dc across.

Rows 4 and 5: Repeat Rows 2 and 3.

All Sizes

Do **not** finish off.

LEFT FRONT

Row 1: Ch 3, turn; skip next sc, (dc, ch 3, dc) in next sc, [skip next 2 sc, (dc, ch 3, dc) in next sc] 4 times, [skip next 2 sc, (hdc, ch 3, hdc) in next sc] 4 times, [skip next 2 sc, (sc, ch 3, sc) in next sc] twice, skip next sc, sc in next sc: 11 dc, 8 hdc, and 5 sc.

Row 2: Ch 1, turn; slip st in first 2 sc and in next ch, ch 1, sc in same sp, (sc, ch 3, sc) in next ch-3 sp, (hdc, ch 3, hdc) in next 4 ch-3 sps, (dc, ch 3, dc) in next 5 ch-3 sps, dc in last dc: 11 dc, 8 hdc, and 3 sc.

Row 3: Ch 3, turn; (dc, ch 3, dc) in next 5 ch-3 sps, (hdc, ch 3, hdc) in next 4 ch-3 sps, hdc in next ch-3 sp: 11 dc and 9 hdc.

EXTRA LARGE, 2X, AND 3X BODY ASSEMBLY

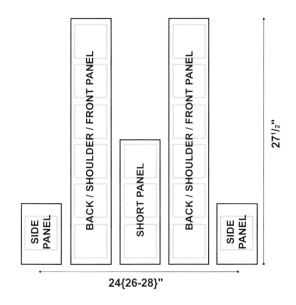

SIDE PANEL

BACK / SHOULDER / FRONT PANEL

SHORT PANEL

BACK / SHOULDER / FRONT PANEL

SIDE PANEL

27¹/₂"

24{26-28}"

SMALL, MEDIUM, AND LARGE

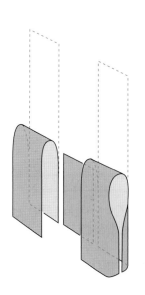

EXTRA LARGE, 2X, AND 3X

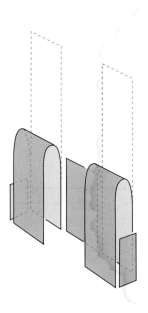

Row 4: Ch 1, turn; slip st in first 2 hdc and in next ch, ch 2 **(counts as hdc)**, (hdc, ch 3, hdc) in next 3 ch-3 sps, (dc, ch 3, dc) in next 5 ch-3 sps, dc in last dc: 11 dc and 7 hdc.

Sizes Small, Extra Large, and 2X Only
Finish off.

Sizes Medium, Large, and 3X Only
Row 5: Ch 3, turn; (dc, ch 3, dc) in next 7 ch-3 sps, hdc in last ch-3 sp: 15 dc and 1 hdc.

Row 6: Ch 1, turn; slip st in first 2 sts and in next ch, ch 2, (dc, ch 3, dc) in next 6 ch-3 sps, dc in last dc: 13 dc and 1 hdc.

Sizes Medium and 3X Only
Finish off.

Size Large Only
Row 7: Ch 3, turn; (dc, ch 3, dc) in next 5 ch-3 sps, hdc in last ch-3 sp: 11 dc and 1 hdc.

Row 8: Ch 1, turn; slip st in first 2 sts and in next ch, ch 2, (dc, ch 3, dc) in next 4 ch-3 sps, dc in last dc.

Finish off.

RIGHT FRONT
Row 1: With **right** side facing, join yarn with slip st in first st of Long Panel edging on right front; ch 3, skip next sc, (dc, ch 3, dc) in next sc, [skip next 2 sc, (dc, ch 3, dc) in next sc] 4 times, [skip next 2 sc, (hdc, ch 3, hdc) in next sc] 4 times, [skip next 2 sc, (sc, ch 3, sc) in next sc] twice, skip next sc, sc in next sc: 11 dc, 8 hdc, and 5 sc.

Complete same as Left Front, beginning with Row 2.

WAISTBAND AND PEPLUM
Row 1: With **right** side facing and working in end of rows, join yarn with sc in Left Front corner; work {140-152-164} {188-194-200} sc evenly spaced across to Right Front corner: {141-153-165}{189-195-201} sc.

Row 2: Ch 4 **(counts as first dc plus ch 1, now and throughout)**, turn; skip next sc, dc in next sc, ★ ch 1, skip next sc, dc in next sc; repeat from ★ across: {71-77-83}{95-98-101} dc.

Row 3: Ch 1, turn; sc in each dc and in each ch across: {141-153-165}{189-195-201} sc.

Row 4: Ch 1, turn; sc in each sc across.

Rows 5-10: Repeat Rows 2-4 twice.

Row 11: Ch 3, turn; skip next sc, ★ (dc, ch 3, dc) in next sc, skip next 2 sc; repeat from ★ across, dc in last sc: {94-102-110}{126-130-134} dc and {46-50-54}{62-64-66} ch-3 sps.

Rows 12 thru {23-23-23}{25-25-25}: Ch 3, turn; (dc, ch 3, dc) in each ch-3 sp across, dc in last dc.

Do **not** finish off.

FINISHING EDGE

Row 1: Ch 1, working in end of rows of Waist and Peplum and in sts on Left Front and Right Front edges, sc evenly across to lower corner of Left Front.

Rows 2 and 3: Ch 1, turn; sc in each sc across.

Finish off.

SLEEVE
FILLER ROWS

Row 1: With **right** side facing, working in back loops only of Rnd 3 of Border on one Short Panel, join yarn with sc in bottom right corner ch; sc in each st across to next corner, sc in corner ch: 61 sc.

Sizes Extra Large, 2X, and 3X Only
Row 2: Ch 1, turn; sc in each sc across.

All Sizes
Next Row: Ch 3, turn; (dc, ch 1, dc) in next sc, ★ skip next 2 sc, (dc, ch 1, dc) in next sc; repeat from ★ across to last 2 sc, skip next sc, dc in last sc: 42 dc and 20 ch-1 sps.

Next {2-2-2}{3-3-3} Rows: Ch 3, turn; (dc, ch 1, dc) in each ch-1 sp across, dc in last dc.

Last Row: Ch 1, turn; skip first dc, sc in each dc and in each ch across; finish off: 61 sc.

Repeat on remaining {3-3-3} {5-5-5} Short Panels.

SLEEVE ASSEMBLY
With **wrong** sides of Short Panels together, bottom edges at same end and working through inside loops, whipstitch {2-2-2}{3-3-3} Short Panels together **(see Sleeve Assembly Diagrams, page 29)**.

Repeat for second Sleeve.

BOTTOM EDGING

Rnd 1: With **right** side facing, join yarn with sc in any joining; work {59-59-59}{98-98-98} sc evenly spaced around; join with slip st to first sc, finish off: {60-60-60}{99-99-99} sc.

TOP EDGING

Sizes Small, Medium, and Large Only

Work same as Bottom Edging.

Sizes Extra Large, 2X, and 3X Only

Rnd 1: With **right** side facing, join yarn with sc in any joining; work 99 sc evenly spaced around; join with slip st to first sc, finish off: 100 sc.

SLEEVE CUFF

Rnd 1: With **right** side facing, join yarn with slip st in any sc on Bottom Edging; ch 4, dc in same st, skip next 2 sc, ★ (dc, ch 1, dc) in next st, skip next 2 sts; repeat from ★ around, join with slip st to first dc: {40-40-40}{66-66-66} dc and {20-20-20}{33-33-33} ch-1 sps.

Rnds 2-5: Slip st in next ch-1 sp, ch 4, dc in same sp, (dc, ch 1, dc) in each ch-1 sp around: join with slip st to first dc.

Last {2-2-2}{4-4-4} Rnds: Slip st in next ch-sp, ch 6 **(counts as first dc plus ch 3)**, dc in same sp, (dc, ch 3, dc) in each ch-sp around; join with slip st to first dc.

Finish off.

Repeat for second Sleeve.

Whipstitch Top Edging of Sleeves into Sleeve openings.

Sew buttons to left edge of Waist on Rows 2, 5, and 8, using ch-1 sp at right edge of same row as buttonhole.

Design by Tammy Hildebrand.

SMALL, MEDIUM, AND LARGE SLEEVE ASSEMBLY

14"

20½"

SLEEVE PANEL

SLEEVE PANEL

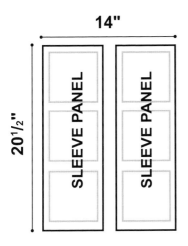

EXTRA LARGE, 2X, AND 3X SLEEVE ASSEMBLY

22"

22"

SLEEVE PANEL

SLEEVE PANEL

SLEEVE PANEL

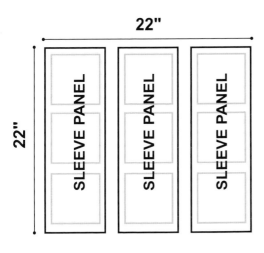
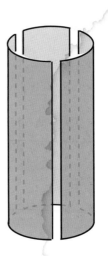

General Instructions

ABBREVIATIONS

ch(s)	chain(s)
cm	centimeters
dc	double crochet(s)
dec	decrease
hdc	half double crochet(s)
mm	millimeters
Rnd(s)	Round(s)
sc	single crochet(s)
sp(s)	space(s)
st(s)	stitch(es)
tr	treble crochet(s)
YO	yarn over

★ — work instructions following ★ as many **more** times as indicated in addition to the first time.

† to † — work all instructions from first † to second † **as many** times as specified.

( ) or [ ] — work enclosed instructions **as many** times as specified by the number immediately following **or** work all enclosed instructions in the stitch or space indicated **or** contains explanatory remarks.

colon (:) — the number(s) given after a colon at the end of a row or round denote(s) the number of stitches you should have on that row or round.

GAUGE

Exact gauge is **essential** for proper fit. Before beginning your project, make the sample swatch given in the individual instructions in the yarn and hook specified. After completing the swatch, measure it, counting your stitches and rows or rounds carefully. If your swatch is larger or smaller than specified, **make another, changing hook size to get the correct gauge**. Keep trying until you find the size hook that will give you the specified gauge. Once proper gauge is obtained, measure width of garment approximately every 3" (7.5 cm) to be sure gauge remains consistent.

ZEROS

To consolidate the length of an involved pattern, zeros are sometimes used so that all sizes can be combined. For example, ch 0{1-2} means the first size would do nothing, the second size would ch 1, and the largest size would ch 2.

REVERSE SINGLE CROCHET
(abbreviated reverse sc)
Working from **left** to **right**,
★ insert hook in st to right of
hook **(Fig. 4a)**, YO and draw
through, under and to left of
loop on hook (2 loops on hook)
(Fig. 4b), YO and draw through
both loops on hook **(Fig. 4c)**
(reverse sc made, Fig. 4d);
repeat from ★ around.

Fig. 4a

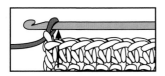

Fig. 4b

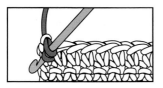

Fig. 4c

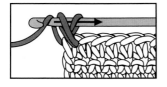

Fig. 4d

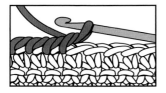

JOINING WITH SC
When instructed to join with
sc, begin with a slip knot on
hook. Insert hook in stitch or
space indicated, YO and pull up
a loop, YO and draw through
both loops on hook.

BACK LOOP ONLY
Work only in loop indicated by
arrow **(Fig. 5)**.

Fig.5

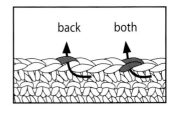

back   both

WHIPSTITCH
Place two Motifs with **wrong**
sides together. Sew through
both pieces once to secure the
beginning of the seam, leaving
an ample yarn end to weave
in later. Insert the needle from
front to **back** through loops
specified in individual instructions
(Figs. 6a & b). Bring the needle
around and insert it from **front** to
back through next loops of both
pieces. Continue in this manner
across, keeping the sewing yarn
fairly loose.

Fig. 6a

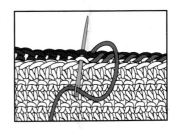

Fig. 6b

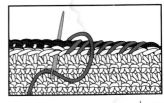

CROCHET HOOKS	
Metric mm	U.S.
2.25	B-1
2.75	C-2
3.25	D-3
3.5	E-4
3.75	F-5
4	G-6
5	H-8
5.5	I-9
6	J-10
6.5	K-10½
9	N
10	P
15	Q

Yarn Weight Symbol & Names	LACE 0	SUPER FINE 1	FINE 2	LIGHT 3	MEDIUM 4	BULKY 5	SUPER BULKY 6
Type of Yarns in Category	Fingering, 10-count crochet thread	Sock, Fingering Baby	Sport, Baby	DK, Light Worsted	Worsted, Afghan, Aran	Chunky, Craft, Rug	Bulky, Roving

CROCHET TERMINOLOGY

UNITED STATES		INTERNATIONAL
slip stitch (slip st)	=	single crochet (sc)
single crochet (sc)	=	double crochet (dc)
half double crochet (hdc)	=	half treble crochet (htr)
double crochet (dc)	=	treble crochet (tr)
treble crochet (tr)	=	double treble crochet (dtr)
double treble crochet (dtr)	=	triple treble crochet (ttr)
triple treble crochet (tr tr)	=	quadruple treble crochet (qtr)
skip	=	miss

■□□□ BEGINNER	Projects for first-time crocheters using basic stitches. Minimal shaping.
■■□□ EASY	Projects using yarn with basic stitches, repetitive stitch patterns, simple color changes, and simple shaping and finishing.
■■■□ INTERMEDIATE	Projects using a variety of techniques, such as basic lace patterns or color patterns, mid-level shaping and finishing.
■■■■ EXPERIENCED	Projects with intricate stitch patterns, techniques and dimension, such as non-repeating patterns, multi-color techniques, fine threads, small hooks, detailed shaping and refined finishing.

We have made every effort to ensure that these instructions are accurate and complete. We cannot, however, be responsible for human error, typographical mistakes, or variations in individual work.

Production Team: Instructional Editor - Joan Beebe; Technical Editor/ Graphic Artist - Liz Field; Editorial Writer - Susan McManus Johnson; Photo Stylist - Angela Alexander; and Photographer - Jason Masters.